First Lessons®

— Alto Saxophone —

by Jeremy Viner

I0812331

Online Audio www.melbay.com/22234BCDEB

Audio Contents

1	Exercise 2-1	17	Exercise 6-1	33	Little Waltz
2	Exercise 2-2	18	Exercise 6-2	34	Staccato Exercise
3	Mary Had A Little Lamb	19	Resting Easy	35	Staccato Waltz
4	Hot Cross Buns	20	No Rest for the Weary	36	The Sorcerer's Apprentice
5	Exercise 3-1	21	All Tied Up	37	Symphony No. 5
6	Exercise 3-2	22	Hold On	38	Musette in D Major
7	Exercise 3-3	23	F Major Tune	39	Minuet in G
8	Exercise 3-4	24	Bb Major Tune	40	Triple Double
9	Exercise 4-1	25	Dot Your I's	41	Swan Lake Waltz
10	Exercise 4-2	26	Dots and Moonbeams	42	Hungarian Dance No. 5
11	Exercise 4-3	27	Three for Me	43	Adagio in G Major
12	Exercise 4-4	28	Two for You	44	Waltz of the Flowers
13	D Major Scale	29	A New Feel	45	Symphony 40 in G Minor
14	Exercise 5-1	30	Can You Hear Me?	46	Spring Song
15	Exercise 5-2	31	Change in the Wind		
16	Exercise 5-3	32	Connect the Dots		

MEL BAY®

1 2 3 4 5 6 7 8 9 0

© 2011 BY MEL BAY PUBLICATIONS, INC., PACIFIC, MO 63069.
ALL RIGHTS RESERVED. INTERNATIONAL COPYRIGHT SECURED. B.M.I. MADE AND PRINTED IN U.S.A.
No part of this publication may be reproduced in whole or in part, or stored in a retrieval system, or transmitted in any form or by any means, electronic, mechanical, photocopy, recording, or otherwise, without written permission of the publisher.

Visit us on the Web at www.melbay.com — E-mail us at email@melbay.com

Introduction

This book is designed to teach both children and adults beginning technique on the alto saxophone as well as basic music reading skills. Exercises are tailored to assist in gradually integrating newly learned techniques. The lessons that follow include basic saxophone technique, music reading skills, and techniques like articulation and dynamics. There are 46 exercises and melodies to help explore the techniques learned in the lessons. These include classical melodies from composers like Bach, Beethoven, Mozart, Tchaikovsky, Schubert, and others. The accompanying audio has examples of all 46 exercises and melodies being played on alto saxophone with piano accompaniment.

Contents

Music Reading Fundamentals

The Staff, Treble Clef, and Measures

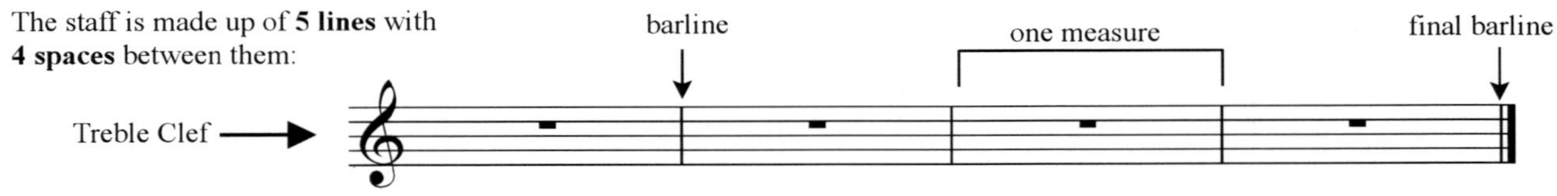

Notes on the Lines

Every Good Boy Does Fine:

Notes on the Spaces

FACE:

4/4 Time Signature and Note Lengths

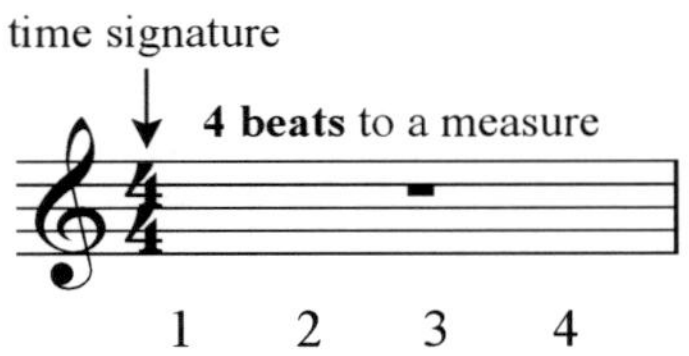

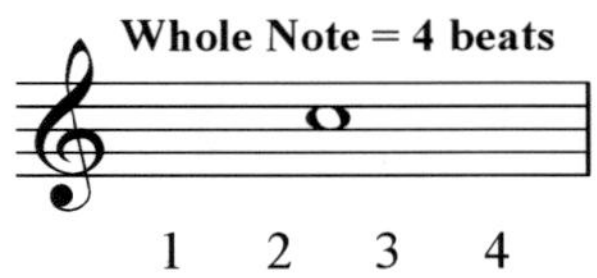

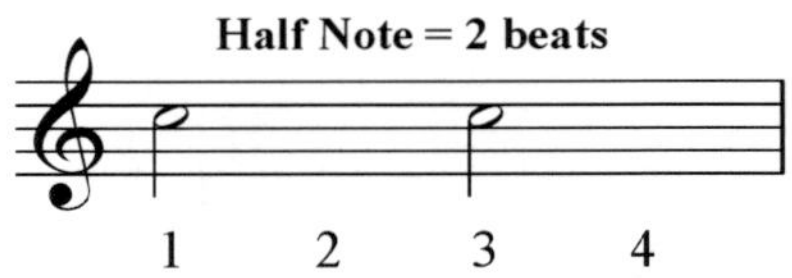

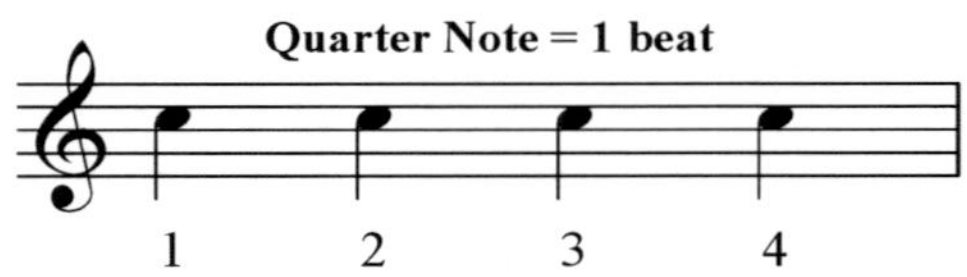

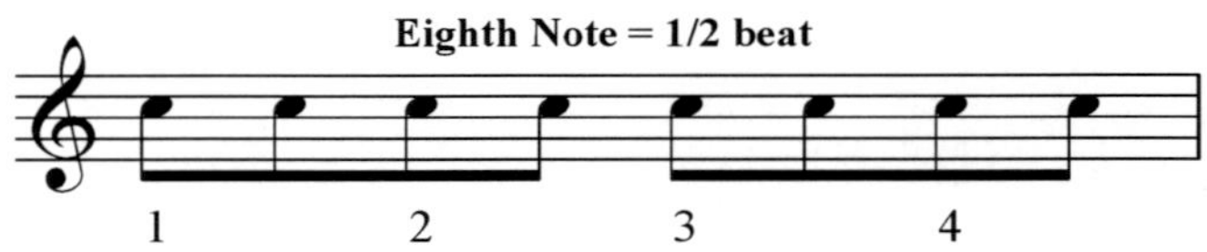

Learning New Notes, Developing Your Sound and Embouchure

The first few lessons will teach you how to play specific notes on the saxophone. The fingerings are coupled with the note as it's seen on the staff as a whole note. When learning these fingerings, play each note for a full breath. To help develop your sound and embouchure (the shape of your mouth around the mouthpiece) try these exercises with each new note you learn:

1) Take a deep breath and play the note until you run out of breath.

2) Take a deep breath, start the note quiet and gradually get louder until you run out of breath.

3) Take a deep breath, start the note loud and gradually get quieter until you run out of breath.

4) Take a deep breath, start the note quiet, get as loud as you can and then get quiet again in one breath.

The Reed and Mouthpiece

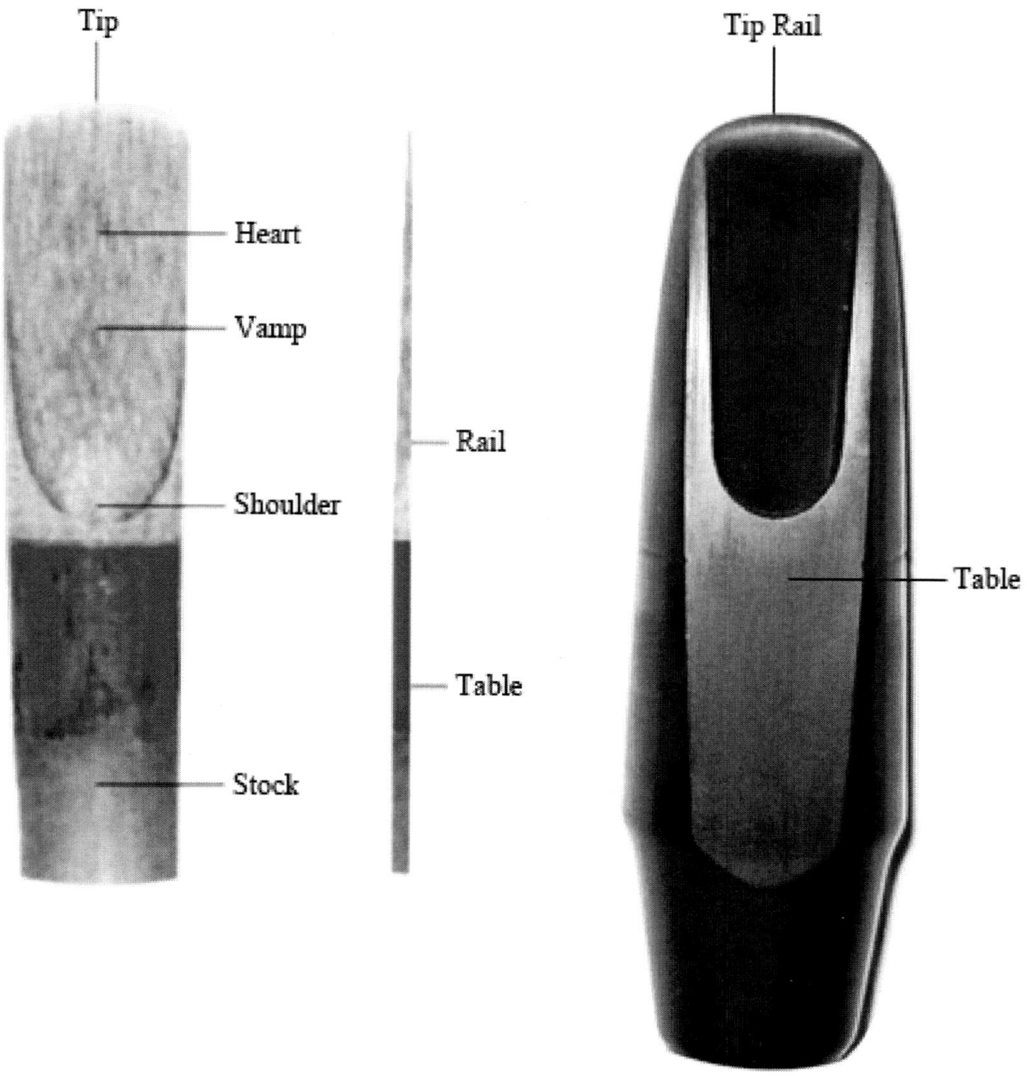

The reed should be secured to the table of the mouthpiece with a ligature. Only tighten the ligature enough so that the reed stays in place. The tip of the reed should line up with the tip of the mouthpiece to create a good seal.

Posture and Breathing

Correct posture is important for breathing and has a direct effect on the sound you produce. Make sure your back and neck are straight when playing and that both of your feet are firmly on the floor. Do not lift or lower your shoulders while breathing. You should try to fill your lungs to capacity when breathing and try to keep your airstream steady when exhaling.

Alto Saxophone Tablature

Here is a visual aid to help in understanding how the saxophone fingerings in this book are represented. The saxophone tablature used is a full graphic representation of the keys on the saxophone. The tablature is laid out as though you were facing the instrument . The left hand fingerings are represented on the top half of the tablature while the bottom half represents right hand fingerings.

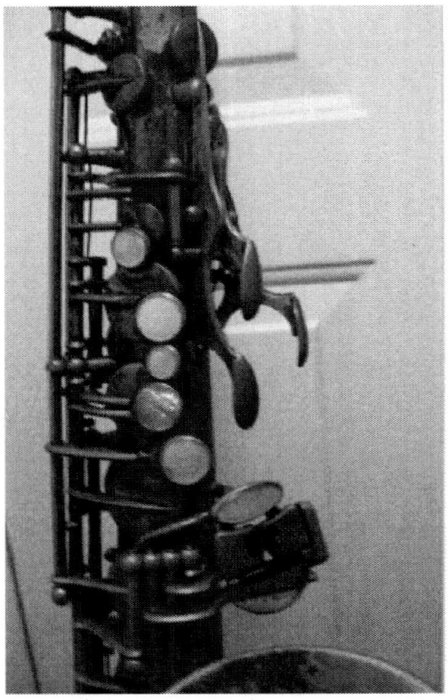

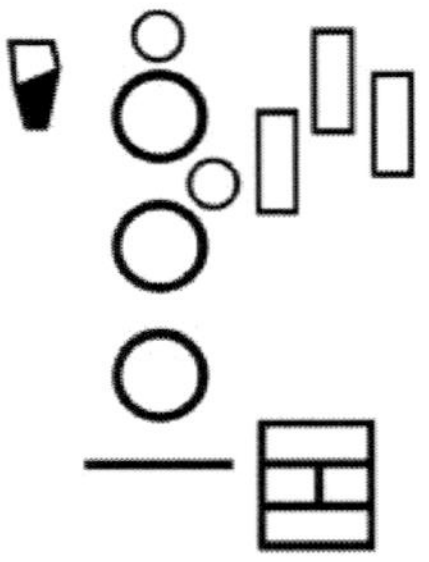

LEFT HAND

The three large cirles on the saxophone tab correspond to where your left index, middle, and ring fingers rest.

The set of four keys below the third finger are all played with the pinky finger. When not being used, it can rest on the top key.

Your thumb should rest on the button under the octave key on the back of the saxophone (in the tablature the left thumb rest is represented in black with the octave key above it).

The three keys on the side of the saxophone are played with the left palm. When not in use your palm should fit comfortably around these keys.

RIGHT HAND

The three large cirles on the saxophone tab correspond to where your right index, middle, and ring fingers rest.

The set of two keys below your third finger are played by the right pinky.

Your right thumb rests under the hook (right thumb rest) on the back of the saxophone.

The three keys on the the right side of the saxophone are played by the right palm.

The key between the second and third fingers is typically played with the third finger though this key is used less frequently.

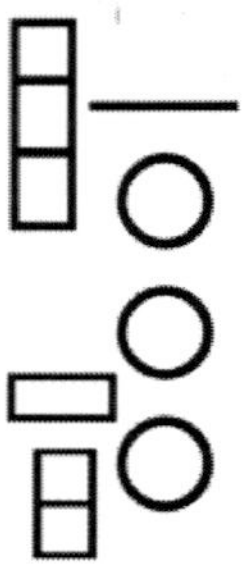

Lesson 1

Assembling and Holding the Saxophone

- First, take out a reed that you can keep in your mouth while putting the instrument together so it will be ready to play.

- Place the neckstrap around your neck and hook the other end to the loop located between the two thumb rests on the back.
- Gently screw your mouthpiece onto the neck's cork, then screw the neck into the body of the instrument.
- Place your reed onto the mouthpiece so that the tip of the reed is aligned with the tip of the mouthpiece. Secure the stock of the reed to the lower half of the mouthpiece with your ligature. The screws on the ligature should be facing right.
- Place your right thumb under the hook on the bottom half of the saxophone and your left thumb on the button below the octave key.
- Adjust the neckstrap so that you are not bending your neck or leaning forward in order to reach the mouthpiece.
- Rest your fingers on the keys as shown above.

Making Your First Sound

Roll your lower lip over your bottom teeth like you are saying the letter "V". The mouthpiece should be about half an inch into your mouth. Rest the reed on your lower lip and close your mouth around the mouthpiece, resting your teeth on top. Put your tongue on the tip of the reed. Take a deep breath and remove your tongue from the reed as you release a steady stream of air.

Lesson 2

First Notes: G, A, and B

Track 1
Exercise 2-1

(breath mark)

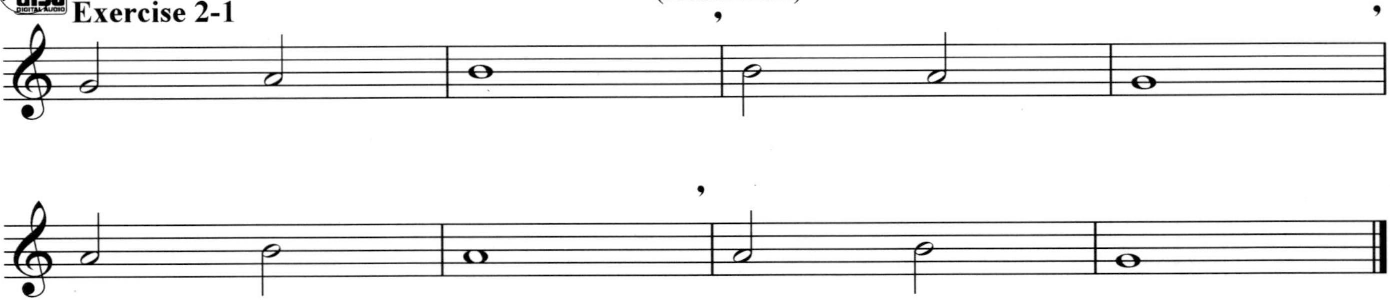

Track 2
Exercise 2-2

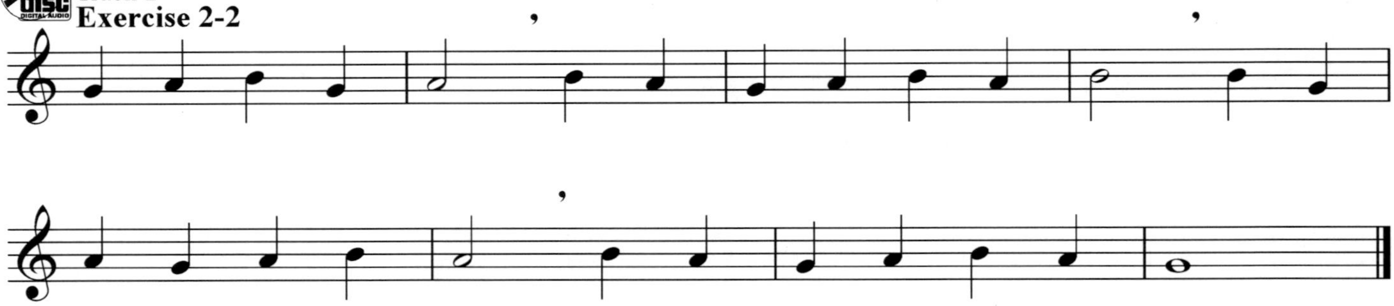

Track 3
Mary Had A Little Lamb

Track 4
Hot Cross Buns

Lesson 3

New Notes: F, E, and D

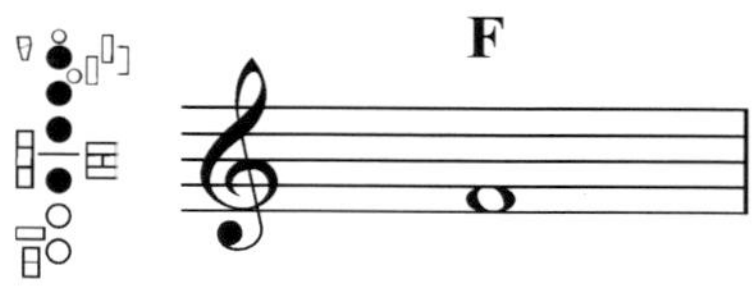

Track 5

Exercise 3-1

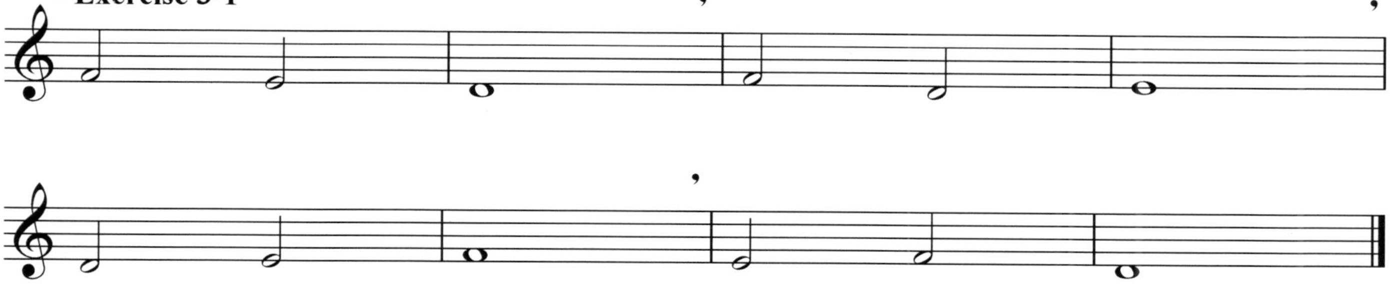

Track 6

Exercise 3-2

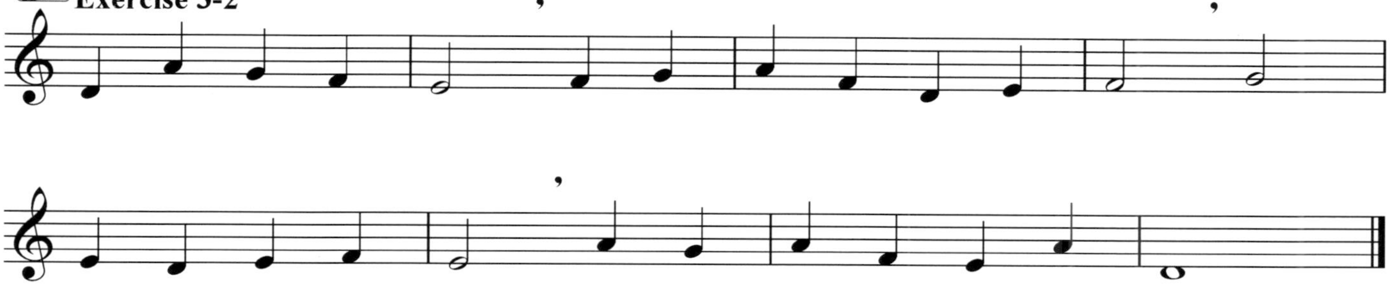

Track 7

Exercise 3-3

Track 8

Exercise 3-4

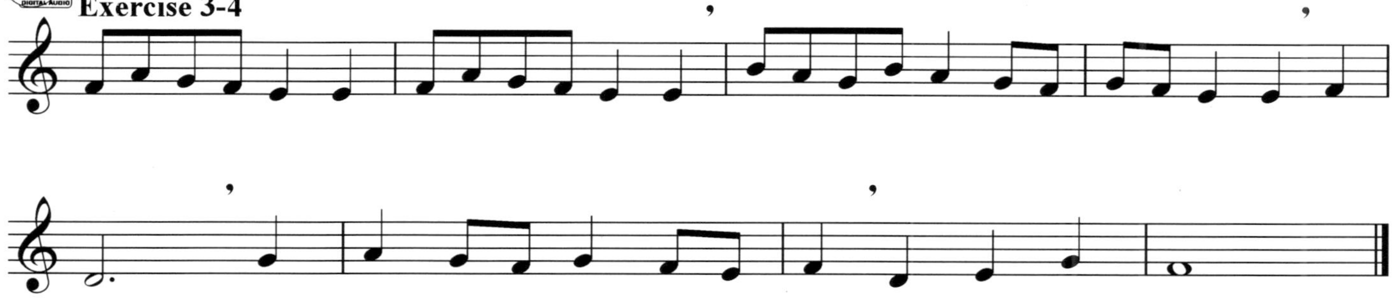

Lesson 4

New Notes: C, Bb, and Ab

C

Bb

Ab

Track 9

Exercise 4-1

Track 10

Exercise 4-2

Track 11

Exercise 4-3

Track 12

Exercise 4-4

Lesson 5

New Notes: F#, C# and Bridging the Octave

Track 13
D major scale

Track 14
Exercise 5-1

Track 15
Exercise 5-2

Track 16
Exercise 5-3

Lesson 6

Ledger Lines and The Upper Octave

Ledger lines are used to aid in reading musical notes that that go above or below the staff.

The **upper octave** is achieved by pressing the **octave key** with your left thumb. The fingerings for the notes in the higher octave are the same as the lower octave with the addition of the octave key:

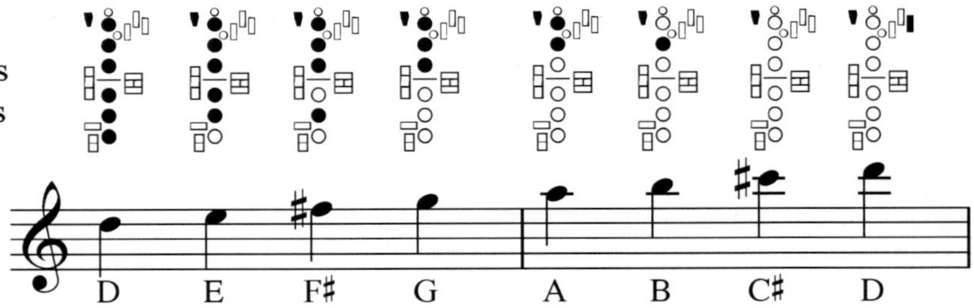

Track 17
Exercise 6-1

Track 18
Exercise 6-2

Lesson 7

Rests

A **whole** rest
is 4 beats.

A **half** rest
is 2 beats.

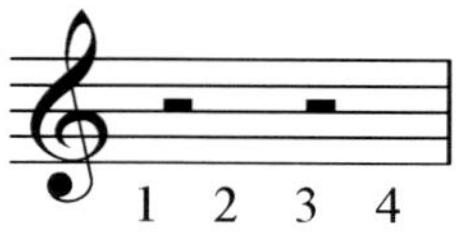

A **quarter** rest
is 1 beat.

There are two **eighth**
rests per beat.

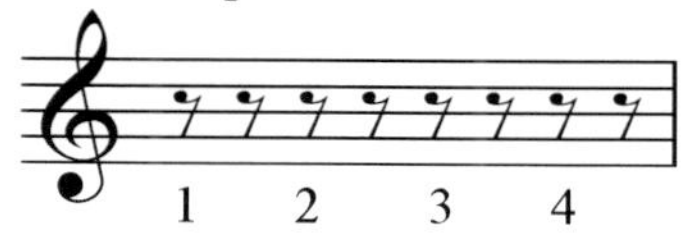

Track 19
Resting Easy

Track 20
No Rest for the Weary

Lesson 8

Ties

A **tie** indicates that a note is to be held to another note. Ties are used to hold notes over from one measure to the next. They can also be used within a measure.

Track 21
All Tied Up

Track 22
Hold On

Lesson 9

Key Signatures

A **key signature** is a placed at the beginning of a piece or section and tells you what **sharps** or **flats** will be used in the piece or section. The following key signature means that all the **F**'s and **C**'s will be **sharp** in the music that follows unless noted otherwise (with a natural sign).

Now let's try the key of **F Major**. There is one flat in F Major - **Bb**. Make sure when you see a 'B' that you remember to play **Bb** instead.

Track 23
F Major Tune

Eb is similar to the fingering for **D** with the addition of your right pinky. The higher octave can be achieved by adding the octave key (left thumb).

Here is the fingering for **Eb:**

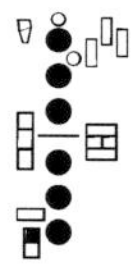

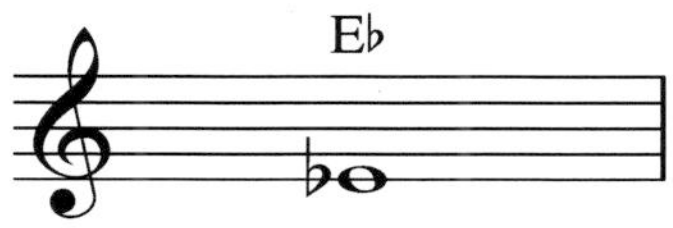

Now let's try the key of **Bb Major**. There are two flats in Bb Major - **Bb** and **Eb**.

Track 24
Bb Major Tune

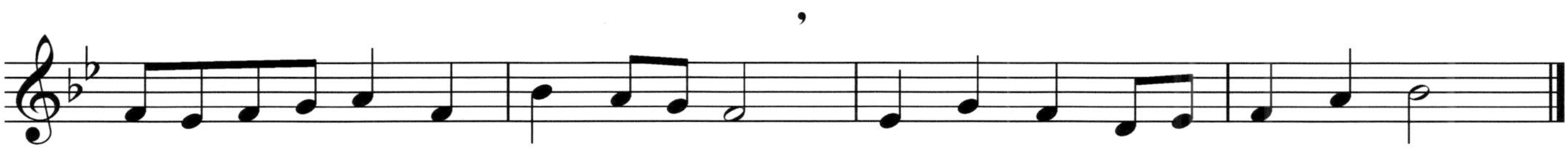

Lesson 10

Dotted Rhythms

When a **dot** is added to a note/rest, it **lengthens** that note/rest by **half** the value of that note/rest:

a **dotted half** note is three **quarter** notes long

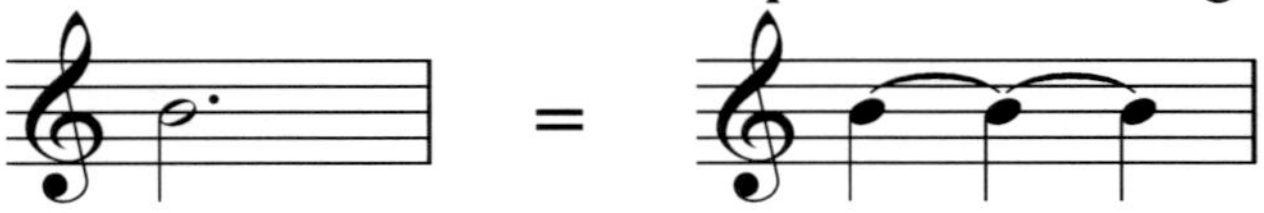

a **dotted half** rest is three **quarter** rests long

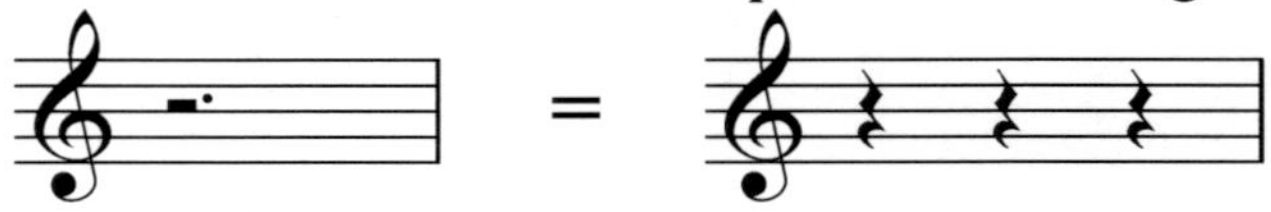

a **dotted quarter** note is three **eighth** notes long

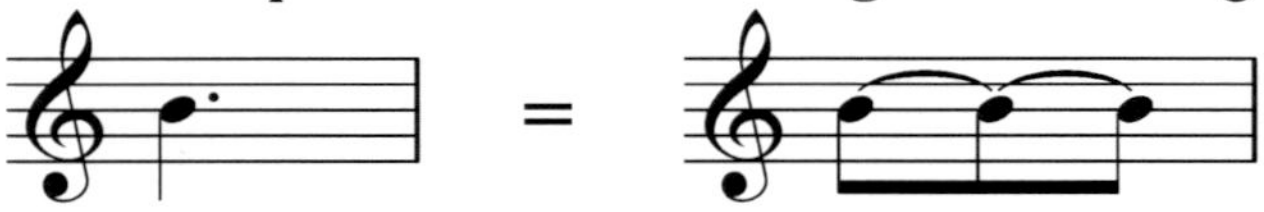

a **dotted quarter** rest is three **eighth** rests long

Track 25

Dot Your I's

Track 26

Dots and Moonbeams

Lesson 11

New Time Signatures: 3/4, 2/4, and 6/8

The top number of a time signature describes how many beats are in the measure. The bottom number describes what note value receives one beat. In **3/4** there are **3 beats** per measure and each beat is one **quarter** note in length. In **2/4** there are **2 beats** per measure and each beat is on **quarter** note in length. In **6/8** there are **6 beats** per measure and each beat is one **eighth** note in length.

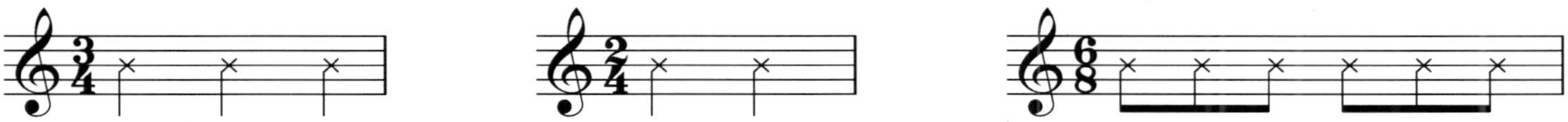

Track 27

Three for Me

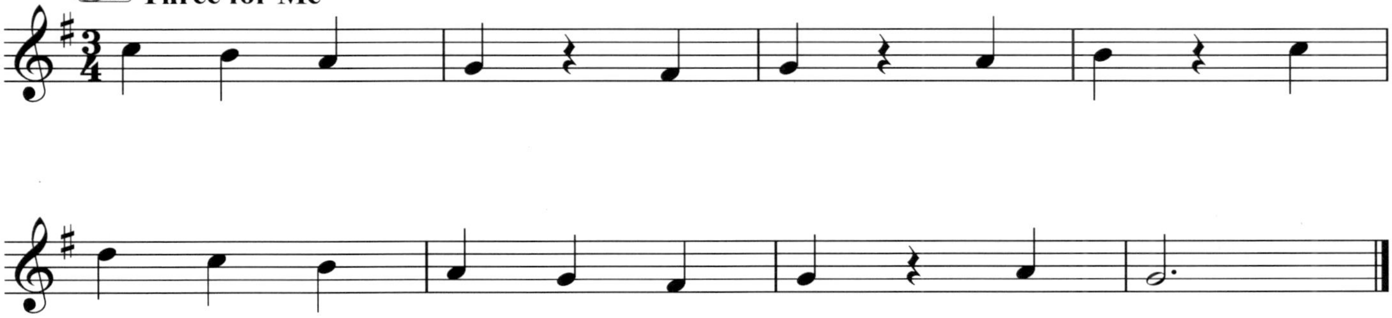

Track 28

Two For You

Track 29

A New Feel

Lesson 12

Dynamics

Dynamic markings are used to indicate how soft or loud the music should be played. You can control your dynamics by adjusting how much air you use.

pp pianissimo very soft	***p*** piano soft	***mp*** mezzo piano medium soft	***mf*** mezzo forte medium loud	***f*** forte loud	***ff*** fortissimo very loud

Track 30

Can You Hear Me?

Crescendos mean to play gradually louder while **decrescendos** mean to play gradually softer.

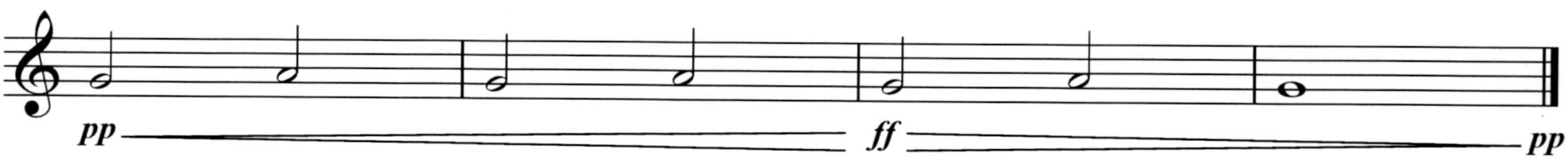

Track 31

Change in the Wind

Lesson 13

Slurs

Slurs look similar to ties but instead of connecting two of the same note, a slur connects two or more different notes. Slurs are used to show a composer's intent regarding phrasing. Instead of attacking each note with your tongue, play each note in the slur with one steady breath.

Track 32
Connect the Dots

Track 33
Little Waltz

Lesson 14

Staccato

Staccato tonguing is a method of tonguing where notes are played short with gaps in between. Staccato notes are notated with a little dot above or below the notehead. To produce staccato notes, start the note with your tongue and then stop it with your tongue after the note sounds.

Track 34
Staccato Exercise

Track 35
Staccato Waltz

Lesson 15

Accents

Accents are used to indicated that a pitch is to be played louder than others. You can achieve the accent effect by starting the note with your tongue and using a small burst of air. Accents are notated with an **accent mark (>)** above or below the notehead.

Track 36

The Sorecer's Apprentice

Paul Dukas

Track 37

Symphony No. 5

Ludwig van Beethoven

Lesson 16

Sixteenth Notes

Sixteenth notes are twice as fast as eighth notes. While eighth notes have one beam connecting them, sixteenth notes have two. Here are some examples of what sixteenth notes look like on their own and in groups:

Track 38

Musette in D Major

J.S. Bach

Lesson 17

Repeats

Repeats are used to show that a musical section should be played twice. Repeat signs come in pairs. There is an **start repeat sign** at the beginning of the musical section and an **end repeat sign** at the end. The music in between the repeat signs is played **two times**. After the second time through the section, move on to the next section.

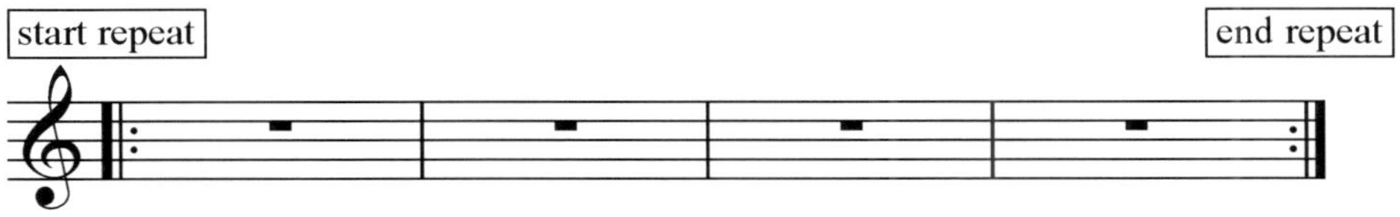

In *Minuet in G*, there are two sections. Both have repeat signs so make sure you play both sections **twice**!

Minuet in G Track 39

J.S. Bach

Lesson 18

Triplets

Triplets divide the beat into three even parts. There are two ways triplets are notated. If all three notes of an eight note triplet are to be played then the triplet is notated with a small **3** above or below the beam of the eigth notes. If one of the notes is replaced with a rest then a bracket is drawn above or below the three parts of the triplet and a small **3** is placed in the center of that bracket.

A **triplet** means that three notes are to be played in the space of two. An eighth note triplet takes place in the space of two eighth notes (or one quarter note):

Track 40
Triple Double

Lesson 19

1st and 2nd Endings

Composers will often use **1st** and **2nd endings** in cases where sections of music are repeated but have slight variations in their endings. In this example, the **1st ending** starts at the beginning of the last line of the page. Play through to the repeat sign like you normally would. On the second time through the repeated section, skip those first two measures of the last line and go directly to the **2nd ending**.

Track 41

Swan Lake Waltz

Pyotr Ilyich Tchaikovsky

Hungarian Dance No. 5

Johannes Brahms

Adagio in G Major

Franz Schubert

Track 43

Waltz of the Flowers

Pyotr Ilych Tchaikovsky

Symphony 40 in G Minor

Wolfgang Amadeus Mozart

Track 45

Spring Song

Felix Mendelssohn

p
p
p
f
f
p
p

Alto Saxophone Fingering Chart